Pétrole

Steph Pike is a feminist socialist activist and a committee member of Manchester People's Assembly, part of the national movement against cuts and austerity. Her poetry has been published in numerous anthologies and she has performed extensively across the country, including at many left wing and feminist demos and rallies, produced 5 minute word portraits as part of a human photo booth, and organised guerrilla poetry protests.

Eloquent, volatile and wise, this is a collection that refuses to be suffocated by fashion, definition, body fascism and 'straitjacket calm'. Steph Pike's poems are like that one person at the party you know you can have a real conversation with.
— *Helen Mort, Derbyshire Poet Laureate & Leeds Cultural Fellow*

Steph Pike is indeed a pétroleuse of furious, exquisite, necessary language: setting fires of declamation for those stripped of their voice and unmasking patriarchy's creeping dystopian gaze by poking it eloquently in the eye. Pike reclaims a view of the world with sun-glinting love poems; with narrative landscapes, both urban and wild, that zoom in to the joy of nature's detail; and intuitive ekphrasis heralding women artists otherwise obscured by conspiracies of silence. *Pétroleuse* offers a distinct glimpse, a world-view seen by fiercely clear-seeing eyes, and a voice shaped by Pike's generous, compassionate heart and by confident, powerful sexuality:

> "...we pull each other into cubicles
> agile as otters, in this small space
> we make the cracked walls noble..."

Despite its delicious grit, *Pétroleuse* speaks reassurance; by its generous invitation to experience the joy of casting beautiful light into the darkest shadows, of weeding patriarchy out from where it grips and melting its frozen, loveless heart.
— *Lucy Lepchani, poet, writer & educator*

Steph's poems speak out defiantly, eloquently and passionately against injustice and oppression. She dares to dream of love, rebellion and the meaning of real liberation.
— *Katherine Connelly, author of* Sylvia Pankhurst: Suffragette, Socialist and Scourge of Empire *[Pluto Press]*

Seawater floods the city streets, petrol and sweat scent the air. This is salty back-pocket semaphore, full of fury and love, for all those in need of hope.
— *Michelle Green, author of* Jebel Marra *[Comma Press]*

Steph Pike's exhilarating, brave poetry is a shove towards action and a license to leave safe positions. It is also tender, lyrical and clear. Its insistent rhythms and thought provoking insights have no truck with easy preconceptions; they are an invitation to the voiceless to know they, too, can speak. Prepare to be shaken and stirred.
— *Dr Rebecca Bilkau, poet, playwright & co-founder of Beautiful Dragons Press*

These poems will set your soul on fire just as surely as the Pétroleuses fired Paris in defence of the Commune in 1871. The wealthy were the target then, and they are in the sights of this poet today. Be inspired by these calls to rebellion.
— *Clare Solomon, People's Assembly Against Austerity National Committee & editor of* Springtime: the New Student Rebellions

Also by the author

Full of the Deep Bits [KFS Press]

Pétroleuse

Steph Pike

To Louise,
Lest wishes
Steph
x

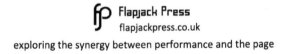 **Flapjack Press**
flapjackpress.co.uk
exploring the synergy between performance and the page

Published in 2016 by Flapjack Press
Salford, Gtr Manchester
flapjackpress.co.uk

ISBN 978-0-9932370-3-4

Front cover image by the author
Design by Brink: paulneads.co.uk

Printed by Lonsdale Direct
Denington Estate, Wellingborough, Northants
lonsdaledirect.co.uk

For my chérie camarade.

Contents

It's easy to feel helpless when confronted with the crushing weight of this world's injustice. To feel overwhelmed; that it's pointless trying any more.

Steph Pike knows it's vital to speak out. That the cost of silence is too high.

In this collection, she takes on the world without flinching or compromise. She won't take the status quo for an answer, nor crumbs from any Tory's table. Between the searing opener, 'Deodorised' and the muscular finale of 'I Want To Fuck David Cameron', Pike roars.

Yet it's not all high-octane. She retains compassion, as in 'To My Husband' and 'Angels of Anarchy'; poems that imprint themselves on the memory's retina with an intimate force.

Poet Amy McCauley wants the poetry she reads to be *necessary*. Pike's work fits that bill, with verve, aplomb and empathy.

Come, as she takes us to the edge of what's reasonable, advisable, acceptable. A place where the wind howls and there is no shelter other than each other. Because here, in the words of Char March's 'Ridgewalking',

> "the views
> are bloody marvellous."

Rosie Garland

Les Pétroleuses - the women of Paris who were instrumental in starting the revolt that led to the Paris Commune, the radical, socialist, revolutionary government that ruled Paris from March to May 1871; women who built the commune, organised mass assemblies and debates, promoted feminist ideas, fought, built barricades and fiercely defended the commune. The term Pétroleuse was coined by enemies of the Paris Commune, to discredit the women revolutionaries as un-feminine furies, accused of engulfing Paris in flames at the end of the commune. But radical, revolutionary women are fierce, brave, unruly, angry - they challenge, subvert and reject the constraints of femininity imposed by societies and systems that seek to restrict and subjugate them. This book honours and stands shoulder to shoulder with all women - past, present and future - who fight for a better world, for justice, liberation, revolution. For "well-behaved women seldom make history" * - we are all les Pétroleuses. Poetry is part of our struggle. Poetry is a coming together, a communication of our pain, our anger, our hopes, our dreams; it contributes to a collective consciousness - a dream of a fairer world, and a belief that we can turn those dreams into reality. And it is a call to action, to question and change the world we live in. It is a call to take to the streets to fight for what we believe in. To change the world we need words and deeds; words on the page, on the microphone, the megaphone, on placards and banners, words that provoke discussions, debate, ideas and dreams. Words as petrol bombs that explode us into activism.

Steph Pike

---

* Laurel Thatcher Ulrich

Pétroleuse

We Will Not Be Deodorised

take your shackles, your chains
your violence, your rape
we will not be bound
by your laws, your lies
your prejudice, your expectations
your science, your biology
your definitions of who we should be
we create our own lives, our own worlds
we make solid our own outlandish dreams
we are free

take your fashion, your body fascism
your plucking and shaving
your surgery, your plastification
take your perfumed pants
your intimate wipes
your scented sanitary wear
we rejoice in fat and muscle and hair
we stink of blood and sweat and skin
we will not be deodorised
we reek of the ocean deep hot hunger of our lovers' cunts
we will not smell of the sterile chemistry of your misogyny

you shoot us, sedate us
imprison us, terrorise us
refuse to educate us
but still we speak out
still we sing out
still we shout out
we will not be silenced
we are unquiet

across centuries
across borders
we rise up
we fight back
we are dirty
we are brave
we are dangerous
we are pussies and we riot

The Grass is Greener

no more noses pressed against the window
no more backs against the wall
no more fists chasing us away
no more being moved on by the law
instead, an open door
the sweet *ting ting* of the
bell as we walk in
we were out and proud
now we're proud and inside
but something's not quite right
this is one shop but it's got two sides;
one counter for your kind
and another one for mine

on my side
the shrimps are a faded kind of pink
the white mice limp
the space dust doesn't
rock the roof of my mouth, it just splutters
the sherbet fountain stutters then stops
the bubblegum's got no pop
the jelly babies have lost the plot
and when I ask for something special
like Ferrero Rocher
they're suddenly out of stock

I never liked sweets anyway
your candyfloss is suffocating
your cherry lips kiss like Zyclon B
I never wanted things your way
once I used to shoplift
now I have to pay

we used to walk the wild side
now we toe the line
and I know we've come a long way
but I miss my life of crime

Monster

against the towering bergs
I am proportionate
storm petrel, fluid as the sea
orca, solid as ice
no longer gargantuan
I am becalmed
the bitter air soothes my fever
the delicacy of snowflakes restores me
clings to my lumpen cheeks
adorns me
everything that was cracks and drifts away
I melt into the dark abyss
you remain;
Frankenstein
flotsam
bringer of death

it was the year of that dress;
a lemon-meringue mess
of yellow nylon
and white lace trim

in that dress
she was not the girl
who bent a paperclip
and felt the whip of your hand
on her face

in that dress
she was not the girl
who threw her first punch
and heard the satisfying crunch
of her sister's nose

in that dress
she was not the girl
you chased with a belt
and who, for the first time,
smelt her own fear

in that dress
she was not the girl
who disappointed your days
with her strange
and awkward ways

in that dress
she was all things nice
sugar and spice

her mother's pride
the apple of her daddy's eye

in that dress
she was straitjacket calm
good as gold
with folded arms and knees closed
who tried and tried to please

she was your bee's knees

that was the year;
a little girl
in a bile-yellow dress
waiting to explode

Mardi Gras

when I see the 'Fish 'n' Chips and PG Tips'
stall roll into town
I know it's time to dust down
my lesbian uniform
to get a funky crop
on the top of my head
perfect for copping off with women
whose faces I won't recognise
and names I won't remember
by the end of Monday night
I'll put on my favourite combats
with all its pockets and zips
where I'll hide the stash of
coke and Es and whizz
that I'll need to ignore
the army of straights
who've invaded our space;
that I'll need to cheer the parade
and laugh and clap
as they throw their corporate tat
and to believe that I do really look great in my
'Barclays Loves Gay Bankers' baseball cap
and I'll need more drugs just to
cope once again with Hazel Dean
and the endless stream
of Z-list celebs scrambling on stage
for their sweet piece of the Mardi Gras' cake
because someone's found the pot of gold
at the end of our rainbow nation's
weekend extravaganza of
capitalist exploitation and I wonder
is *this* what it was for?

is this why we protested
marched on the streets
got spat on
and arrested?
is this what happened to Gay Liberation
our dreams lying in a Canal Street gutter
buried in rubbish and cold chips
bleeding hope
stinking of puke and stale piss

we're getting civvied up
we're de-mob happy
the war is through
we're rushing out
to say *I do, I do!*
we're very nearly
just like you
we're in the suburbs
with our 4x4s and 2.2
kids, we go on family trips
to International Ladies' Day
hey, times have changed
we've won the right
to become racist thugs in blue
to butch it up in prisons
swing our keys
clank our chains
join the army
we're in the main-
stream now
we're getting carried away
we're celebrating this freedom we've found
with our beautiful, shiny, pink pound
we're pushing out the boat
we're afloat at last
are we fuck
we're all at sea
because this isn't a war that we won
we just crossed over to the enemy

Neon

fireflies, will o' the wisp
ghosts on your retina
night snaps out our words

we talk salty back pocket semaphore
code knocked out on
anonymous doors we inhabit

clubs, back alley, underground
pumping hearts searching
for a way back

to the stars, we sip cocktails
delicate as humming birds inhale
from cistern tops and strangers' keys

our blood floods with music
we dance sublime until
so hot, so wanting

we pull each other into cubicles
agile as otters, in this small space
we make the cracked walls noble

mouths, liquid fingers
unclothing molten cores
the sweat-swilled floor shakes

as dawn breaks, the earth can barely contain us
we are too volatile
we scatter like mercury

To My Husband

After Marion Adnams's painting The Living Tree *[1939].*

that was that
church ding-dong
mask up
game on
kitchen sink and bedroom canapés
dolled up, drilled in, dumbed down
this is what you saw:
a dress, a smile
a knife and fork
talk - what did you hear
here's your drink
nice day dear
and me; a glass
a vessel, a cup of tea

it wasn't real
I've hung up your
heavy gold cutlery
let the mask fall
shed my skin
slipped away
don't look
you'll never find me
you'll see what
you always saw;
a mask
a paper silhouette
a dead tree

A Scuttle of Fur

a scuttle of fur
in the corner of an isle
fern fronds sweat fisheye drops of dew
reflect empty sky
edged by an eagle
elevating itself beyond reason
on the same latitude
a helicopter hovers
its one raptor's eye
pinning our world
into an iron bar grid
with no green canopy
to protect our fledgling lives

Day Trippers

gulls shriek
we burst onto the seafront
hearts juddering like bus engines
laughing we shovel crisps into
mouths too ravenous to shut
against the blowing sand

blue melts into yellow
the end of the summer
washes our backs with warmth
your fingers rippling my hair

later you dribble alien
words and someone else's
half-eaten spring roll into my ear
and I know we're
on the slow train home
half-cut and happy

because both birds and whales sing
I lie down and let you run through me
you sing with
anarchy in your face
my eyes flicker like
side show freaks and
eclipse the setting sun
your anarchy enfolds me
a storm blue sky
where I migrate
to shaking winds
to pods of whales
to fleeting birds
to me

Fly

gannet massive
bigging themselves up
for the high dive down
fly
it beats lying in bed with a hangover
Sunday - bright sunshine, breezy
win! win! win!
an eagle elevates itself
on a thermal high
Arran has a drug problem
surf war
the shore Lamlashed
Can You Help?
quack commandos and seabird reserves
it's in everyone's interest

She Shanty

she anchored her feet on the ocean's deep floor
she salted her locks and the wild winds roared
her shoulders built waves four score fathoms high
the green northern lights were the sweep of her eye

she grasped fast on the manes of the waves' white steeds
her muscles rippling with power and speed
she threw back her head to call up a storm
and shiver me timbers, the salty sea swarmed

brought forth orcas and sharks and shrimps in a squall
all manner of creature heeded her call
they swam and they surfed and they shoaled to her side
starfish and mussels arrived with the tide

they sat round the fire of anemones' glow
tall stories they told and rum it did flow
urchins inked nautical art on her skin
she danced with the fish with gold hoops in their fins

and their laughter gave oceans their heave and their ho
their laughter gave oceans their heave and their ho

The End of the World

After Leonor Fini's painting Le Bout du Monde *[1948/1949].*

volcano sky
crows circle
shark words
outcast rebel
I rise beneath
my nylon wreath
leaves wither
and worlds end
organic eyes
ocean blue
I use them;
I defy
I accuse

we sit at the back of the bus
sun drunk, connected by smiles
and the electric wire of headphones
we airdrum through the Spanish countryside
the crescendos blurring our hands
spilling clouds of icing sugar
from our bag of breakfast onto our feet
we rock and roll past flat dusty towns
past landscapes glimpsed in each other's eyes
and onward to the place where you
teach me to do handstands in the sea

Spanish River

she stands, cigarette smokes
Spanish river flows
still, past her calves I'd seen
earlier, at the top of her stare
I said something - *ravine* -
had heard her
feel where the stare turns
becoming one of blatant river in the sun
catch her eyes, softening
clear green water
and her two easy boys
relaxed moons
in orbit
warming me

me at her centre
sun on my back she takes me
her slippery skin
under my hands hauling me
a waterfall high through the water
up in the river, *swim* she says
we glide over the clear middle
of a narrow crystal pool
deep as her, rushing river, swimming heart
and my toes full of the deep bits
of nothing but shivers
she gives me this
water high as our thighs
through, always through the clambering
wading, scrambling rocks
the ache in my muscles
bursting with pride of her

following the bigness
arms up, fingers gripping
her shoulders moss-rock rolling
her planting feet thundering water
over our soaking bodies

the edge
and with our shoulders, the choice
she by my side
parting the water
falls like a raindrop in great sheets
like a tear
like life brimming in my eyes
the edge and the turn
and the throw of myself
deep in, through her space
the green clear is all surface
around me silent pools
and she is there
and down becomes us
and with a watching smile
me on a rock
and she on the shore

Frida Kahlo

After Frida Kahlo's painting Self-Portrait with Medallion *[1948].*

I can't see you, prone as I am in bed
so I write and paint on my back
in a halo of lace
or a shroud, staring death in the face

tears on my face
like an icon
but I'm no saint
no stoical saviour

I'm in pain
backbone bent, wounds leaking
I gain nothing
I create despite my suffering

Funeral

clouds shroud the sky
ghost birds turn the moon to sun
we're in custody
her bones rattle through the streets
the earth licks its lips and waits

her guard of honour
shell-shocked soldiers, their dead eyes
tears of dictators
her little boys blue squabbling
over this nation's entrails

Dusk in St Anne's Square

into the trees as a
flock they flew, pink of the
wing, so light like a
flake in a blizzard they blew,
tails the length of the
lingering light, they
rose and they fell, rose and
they fell, 'til as one they
sprang back to the
swallowing night

Early Snow Fall

a cold snap
a sudden drop
the clouds are shivery, unsettled
crystal breath streams
persistent as grief
the flakes are thick and slow
tonight they do not want to land
they whisper against each other
so many of us have fallen
voices lost in the blizzard
white noise, amnesia, cataract

tomorrow
nothing will be the same
the landscape ice-burned
all features gone
the world a silent monochrome
our sins died in the wool
on Christmas morning
the body of a young woman
is found under a layer of snow

Piccadilly Gardens

children play in fluting streams
watched by men whose pants
are cast from cold wrought iron
to hide the tell-tale signs
that unleashed, punch 999
into frantic fathers' minds
who report 'robbery'
their exclusive property
coveted by other men's preying eyes

the green and purple kaleidoscopic clouds
of starlings' swirling evening cabaret
are years gone
replaced by metal birds
that roost with hard unblinking eye
static observers of urban life
the city turned voyeurs' paradise

in the cooling rain
night slides down
shadows shift and slink away
the children move like moths
drawn by bleeping squat machines
dispensing dreams
of fame and unknown wealth
the 10p thrill of a neon pleasure dome
safer here than in their homes

Manslaughters

Based on the evidence given by Victor Tabak at his trial in October 2011 for the murder of Joanne Yeates in Bristol in December 2010. He admitted killing her, but claimed it was manslaughter. He was convicted of murder by a majority of 10 - 2.

it was like this
[he holds his hands outstretched, palms up
like he's in a pulpit not a dock]
I walk past her kitchen window
she catches my eye, flirtatious
the way women do
I knock on her door
she says 'Hello'
green light! I move in for a kiss

the cocktease screams and screams and screams
I have to shut her up
I do what anyone would
I grab her throat, lightly
not tight at all, I barely squeeze
but she's blonde, petite, weak

no, there was no struggle
what? the bruises on her face?
the scratches? the blood?
I don't know, self-inflicted
women are dead devious
she wanted me to look bad

I did go to the supermarket
with her in the boot
I had no choice
my girlfriend would have killed me
if I hadn't got the shopping in

bitch!

I had to leave her there
you don't understand what it was like
her body wouldn't go over that wall
no matter how hard I tried
I was sweating, desperate
I was terrified
[he bows his head
he cries]

Amstetten

In 2008 Elisabeth Fritzl escaped from 24 years of captivity and abuse from her father. The British Press went into overdrive, questioning what it was about Austrian society that could allow such an atrocity to happen.

it was all Julie Andrews and alpine meadows
big cream cakes and rosy-faced people
and blue skies with fluffy clouds
and soft brown cows with clanking bells
and clean air and Edelweiss
all pretty and cosy and nice
until one fine upstanding Austrian man
took his daughter by the hand
and shut her up

Amstetten, hang your head in shame
Austria, hang your head in shame

we've taken the lid off
your chocolate box land
and found your dirty soul

the green of the alpine grass
the blue of the cloudless sky
the child's beaming yellow sun
are too perfect, too bright
their coffee and cake sticks in our throats
the cows are a Greek chorus with bells of doom
we hate their too clean streets
their lawns without a blade of grass mis-placed
a neurotic people in the home of Freud
everything too tidy, too fake
a plastic people programmed for evil

their outrages subterranean
hidden beneath their toy-town houses
and smiling yodelling faces
even the Austrians join in
this national flagellation
police and psychiatrists parading on TV
basking in their 5 minutes of fame
pondering who's to blame for this atrocity
is there something in the post-war
Nazi-loving Austrian psyche

because we're shocked, we're at a loss
we can't understand how this has happened

and I think *bullshit!*
this talk of Austrian blame
is a magician's trick
a sleight of hand
an illusionist's game of misdirection

because I look around me
and I see

women naked in cages
in adult clubs
and women naked on pages
in papers and mags
and nose jobs
and boob jobs
and a nip and
a vaginal tuck
to give men a
perfect fitting fuck
and Daddy giving

his little princess
a long kiss goodnight
and thousands of women abused
in our modern
civilised society
where 95% of rapists
go free

and we don't understand how Amstetten happened

girls in pink
and boys in blue
genders assigned
so we don't get confused
so that boys can be boys
and girls know their place
slag, whore
slapper, cunt
wolf-whistles
and show us your tits
and suck my cock
you fucking bitch

and we don't understand how Amstetten happened

Reclaim the Night

along avenues and boulevards
tree-lined streets and winding roads
down country lanes and muddy tracks
in shadowed alleys and cul-de-sacs
on narrow trails through
lonely woods and urban parks
on short routes, long routes
disused rail routes
across wasteland, parkland
farmland, our land
whether city bright or
dark as the night itself
these streets are ours

walking sober and sedate
or stumbling home late
binge-drunk on alcopops and
off our heads on Class A drugs
in sturdy boots or 6 inch heels
in skirts so short and tops slung low
or wrapped up warm against the cold
glammed up, dressed down
made up, veiled up
on the piss or on the pull
in raucous groups and all alone
these streets are ours

homeless, turning tricks
to meet a mate or just for kicks
to sit beneath the stars and moon
and know that soon
the sun will rise upon us, still alive

because sleep evades us
because a whim takes us
because we choose to go
wherever we like
at any time of day or night
to know the twilight
midnight, dawnlight hours
these streets are ours

Suffragette City

in Alexandra Park
young trees shivered with excitement
they wrote this in their rings;
how their leaves dappled the dawn-light
purple, green and white
to shield her coming and going
how the morning exploded
in a thousand diamante stars
and cactus spines rained up
to embroider 'freedom'
on a sullen Manchester sky

how freedom made bold the hearts
of three women climbing gallery steps
skirts crackling with revolution
pockets deep with rage and rocks
how their missiles ricocheted round walls
daubed with men's smug self-congratulation,
to change the course of *his*-story
to crack the future open for us all

a century and a continent away
you, female trinity, Pussy Riot
rip stagnant cathedral air
with punk-raw hymns of rebellion and defiance
until you are dragged to prison camps
and in your cells, through brutal frozen nights
know this; you are not forgotten
you will never be alone
because whenever and wherever
they try to bring a sister down
a million women rise

Clubbing

poledancing is great exercise, right? and
lapdancing is just girls having sexy fun
    lapdancing clubs outnumber
    rape crisis centres
    three to one

nothing about any of this is right
erotic dancing is women's power car-crashed
pole-wrapped, bodies distorted and cash-strapped
souls slapped, men's eyes glued like traps
demanding *gyrate!*
while women's lives are drowned out
in the dingy thumping bass beat of hate

and my heart would crack
except I know that feminism is a Phoenix
and rises back stronger
each time they pronounce it dead

and I long, *I long*
to break the seals of the sea
so that gentlemen's clubs are drowned in silt
so that starfish flood the land
and dance in wonder by our feet
so that women float majestic like icebergs
down urban highways and suburban streets

Prohibition

Leah Betts drowned
I know; her hair was green
and she had starfish in her eyes

twenty years before her time
she paints with Marc Almond on her palette
and sex dwarves on her mind

you wear her shrunken head
around your neck
and still that thing you call a sofa

chews your legs
while *Crimewatch*
tells you not to dream at night

Ecstasy never beat me to death
in my own home
go on then, one more for the road

Sonnet

heaven slams its rusty gates
the xanthine glow of the neon sign
barks SHUT into the salty faces of the dead
the perished mob is brass bold
defenestrates their treacherous god and
flows behind, a ghostly mist
to seal his fate in grey cement
the family on the patio are oblivious
share pizza and beers, cocooned
in the paraphernalia of a summer afternoon
their limbs entwined in knots
the bricks of their home cling close
to demonstrate the nuclear way is fine
while the reactor nearby coughs death into the air

Forged

urban alchemy
brick walls slur with liquid steel
the hills, clenched like fists, circle
sheep-studded and angry
the sun a bullet hole in the sky
the city cries ice rain
hot and hard as rivets

walking home each night, the same picture
the dead soldier has been informed
deliberate and surgical, a blow to the heart
the electronic wailing of a woman
must shut them down
precision missiles and a spate of
roadside bombs play in the street
the shrug of a cold shoulder

dead

like a winter morning
like a shallow afternoon
like an evening drowned
the government paying tribute
crouches like a cancer
staring through unbreakable glass
grimy with fear, I sing the low moan
of apache helicopters clattering for blood

Angels of Anarchy

After Francesca Woodman's photograph Untitled, Rome, Italy *[1977/1978].*

I've taken this space	I've thrown my face
the apron's gone	the apron's skirt masks me
the clean floor mine for once	the floor rancid all the time
I'm Jesus am I	am I not Satan
or a suicide	or a birth
it's not for you to decide	it's for you to divine
I'm not nailed up here	I'm strung up
by your desire	by your apathy
no sacrificial lamb	a blood sacrifice
strong, I hang by my fingers	weakened, my nails tear
head to one side	my head too heavy for my neck
you think I'm dead	you think I'm happy
or depressed	enjoy this
you're wrong	you're wrong
I'm a bird on a branch	I'm a bird in a cage
an acrobat, a free diver	petrified, a sinking stone
an angel about to take flight	an angel without wings

Bankers

bank, city boys, bank
fiddle with yourselves
while our cities burn
don't think of England
keep your eyes on the
billboard consumer porn
spin the roulette wheel
roll the dice once more
and make your laminated
wipe-clean deals
while condom Cameron
protects you from every
financially transmitted disease

you're banking so hard
you're showering us with austerity
with the biting sleet
of grinding poverty
we're drowning in the fall out
of your billion pound bail out
while you destroy the economy of nations
with your skyscraper decadence
and stock market speculations

so bank, city boys, bank
make the most of the good times
we've got our eyes on your balls
we've taken note
of your dodgy scams
of every 'don't give a damn'
dirty deal you've ever sealed

we've taken account of
every home repossessed
every job lost, every life tossed aside
in the pursuit of the ride of your life

so have another line of coke
drink one more glass of fizz
turn on the TV, lie back
and have one last bank
to images of starving children
and broken communities
because we know what you do
and we're coming
we're coming
we're coming
for you

£53 a Week

On 1st April 2013, as the most sweeping and draconian welfare reforms become law, Iain Duncan Smith, the architect of this cruelty, claims he could live on £53 a week.

his hand closes round
notes and coins, foreign
he doesn't like the dirt
the way it disturbs
the soft line of the wool

£5 on gas and electric
he's brought candles, doesn't watch TV
buys a daily paper, the Times
won't eat much, fat enough
for a week, or more

he can do without
doesn't mind the cold
tells himself boarding school was
harsh, how he cried into his pillow
clutching daddy's credit card

he spends the days
straightening his tie against his own
unease, keeps the curtains closed
doesn't go out, speak to anyone
won't look, doesn't learn a thing

at night he sucks his silver spoon
dips his tongue in his own puddled spit
dreams of quails' eggs, exotic trips
the moon sweeps a slow scan over his silk cocoon
an image beams back; cold, barren, blue

Welfare to Workfare

I'm going to forget
that we're slaves to the 40 hour week
and the minimum wage
so we stay in our place
and the rich stay rich
and get myself a job

I'm going to forget
that I'm black and hassled by racists
and stopped by police on a regular basis
because all they can see
is a drug dealer or terrorist
and get myself a job

I'm going to forget
my mental distress,
the fear, the psychosis
the stigma, the sections
my diagnosis
and get myself a job

I'm going to forget
that my kids bunk off school
run with gangs
play with guns
because I'm never home
and get myself two jobs

I'm going to forget
that I worked 40 years
in a job with low pay
in a job that I hated

for a boss with no conscience
who stole my soul and my pension
and get myself a retirement job

I'm going to forget
that we're fighting a war that we didn't want
in a country that hates us
I'm going to forget the civilian deaths
the flashbacks, the trauma
the soldiers in body bags
and get myself an army job

I'm going to forget
the mines closed down
the shipyards closed down
the factories closed down
the shops closed down
the services cut
that they bailed out the banks
with the money we earned
I'm going to forget my P45
the rationalizing, the downsizing
and the efficiency drives
and get myself an invisible job

I'm going to forget that I'm workless
because they couldn't care less
because they feather their own nests
and I'm going to forget that I've got rights
and instead I'll be grateful
for any crumb from their table
and I'll work myself to death

Bedroom Tax

I saw a mansion shine upon a hill
a hundred rooms or more within its walls
and this I found to be a bitter pill;
no more than three were rattling round its halls
this greed did set my sorry soul a' chill
and over me a burning rage did fall
my city's streets were full with people who
were homeless made to benefit the few

Community Care in This Green and ASBO Land

"ASBO bars suicidal woman from rivers." - The Guardian.

if I could wear
a stupid wig
sit in a high chair
talk a load
of old shit
then maybe
I would just be insanely
rich and label free
but...
that ASBO
nearly did the trick
I was too busy
avoiding exclusion zones
to think of ending it
all
you see, it wasn't
how they said
I wasn't trying to tread
on anybody's toes
cause panic or distress
be ungrateful or even rude
but friendless in this teeming world
I didn't want to be alone
I wanted to die
outside under a kindly sky
I just wanted to be found
quickly not left for months
an undiscovered protein slick
but now I'll have to do it here
in this flat, rank
with my own sour breath

my pain staring back
from this chaos I call home
this is where I'll sit
and carve my future
out
and in case
the long arm of the law
extends beyond death
I'll pin a polite note
to my chest
Thanks for you help and
I'm sorry for the mess

the boys are back in town
jack - jack - jacking their veins with hate
bussed in to tell people
who were born here
who work here, live here, love here
to fucking go home

bussed in, seething with sieg heils
tendons popping
mouths frothing
fists like pistons

too scared to grieve
their broken dreams and shattered lives
too scared to cry
these boys pick fights
with anyone and anything that's different

while the BNP sit swaddled
in the greenrooms of the BBC
drip, drip, dripping their poison
through the radio and TV

at the same time, Muslim youth
who dare to care
that a nation state
rains bombs down on
a Palestinian people
already impoverished and prostrate
protest

throw stones that don't hit anyone
throw bottles that don't hurt anyone

have their homes invaded
are paraded in front of a judge
who hands down a five year stretch

a deterrent, he says
to what? to
the pursuit of liberty, justice and truth?
the exercise of our democratic rights?

these judges who peddle racism
to maintain their power and wealth
who peddle racism for their own gain
these white, privileged, corrupt men
they are England's shame

Kettled

the pigeons feel it first
fling themselves up
disappear, grey puffs of smoke
on the taut violet sky
we fall silent
senses strain
there...
above the traffic's evening yawn
it comes;
the thick beat of aggression
the *drum drum drum*
of baton on shield

a tsunami of visored robots roars
move forward
and we are netted
an industrial trawl
that takes activists, protestors
a few bewildered shoppers
dragged deep from their sandy beds

we are encircled, entrapped, enraged
we swirl and eddy like snowglobe flakes
our chants bounce from mouth to mouth
we catch each others eyes for warmth
try to break out
wait
try to break out
wait

minutes tick like bombs
erupt in a riot of whinnies with flailing hooves

crushed by a wall of horse hair
muscle and filth
with nowhere to go
we become a tangle of elbows and twisted legs
are dispersed into kerbs
into glass panes
into bloodied grit
much later they hand out bottled water
but this is no benign embrace
this is the blue circle of a vindictive bruise
a stranglehold, a tightening noose of threat
but we will not be bullied, broken, scared off

our resolve is strengthened
students, workers
the disenfranchised and dispossessed
the links of common cause are forged
we will be back;
until the tide has turned
until this vicious government falls
in this crucible of repression
revolution is born

I Want to Fuck David Cameron

I want to fuck David Cameron
I want to be the divine Mrs C
I want to tweak his ruddy cheeks
run my fingers through his thinning beige hair
rub my body all over his sliced white-dough physique
I want to wear a twin-set in pastel blue
ride with him on his
environmentally friendly bicycle for two
I'm going to wear a hoody - just so
he'll hug me and fill me with his Tory love
I want to be a single mother
I want to be poor, I want to be needy
anything so he'll use me
in a moving photo opportunity
oh yes Davey, my new Tory mate
I really thought you'd turned me straight... except
I want to fuck Margaret Thatcher too
I saw her down Lash for Lasses
suited and booted with her concrete hair and that
'come to bed or I'll break your fucking neck' stare
oh, those Tories have got me so wet
they've gone all lovey-dovey, touchy-feely
they are such sexy Dulux dogs
they've gone all blue with a hint of green
blue with a hint of pink
blue with a hint of black
blue with a hint of any fucking tint
that'll lure those voters' little kisses in
you see they've got me all confused
I used to know where I stood;
the evil Tories were bad
and the LibDems were kind of sort of good

but now they've all merged
into one head-fuck toxic mix
of rightwing, capitalist, war-mongering, poverty making
welfare hating NHS breaking bunch of shits
and I'm so loved up that all I want to do is give
each and every one of them a great big Kirby kiss

Acknowledgements

Versions of 'Age 7', 'Mardi Gras', 'Civil Partnerships and All That Jazz', 'Day Trippers', 'Arran', 'Spanish River', 'Piccadilly Gardens', 'Amstetten', 'Reclaim the Night', 'Clubbing', 'Prohibition', 'Sonnet', 'War on Terror', 'Angels of Anarchy', 'Kettled' and 'I Want to Fuck David Cameron' were first published in *Full of The Deep Bits* [KFS Press, 2010].

'The Grass is Greener' and 'Palma to Port de Pollença' were first published in *Loose Muse: An Anthology of New Writing by Women*, ed.s Sara-Mae Tuson, Chikodi Nwaiwu & Agnes Meadows [Morgan's Eye Press, Spring 2013].

'A Scuttle of Fur' and 'She Shanty' were first published in *Loose Muse: An Anthology of New Writing by Women*, ed.s Sara-Mae Tuson, Chikodi Nwaiwu & Agnes Meadows [Morgan's Eye Press, Autumn 2013].

'Fly' was first published in *Best of Manchester Poets, Vol. 3*, ed.s Cathy Bryant, Steve O'Connor, Angela Smith & Keir Thomas [Puppywolf, 2013].

'Forged' was first published in *Sculpted Poetry of the North West*, ed.s Lindsey Holland & Angela Topping [North West Poets, 2013].

'Bankers' was first published in *Poems for Freedom*, ed. Alex Clarke [Freedom Press, 2013].

'Monster' was first published in *Loose Muse: An Anthology of New Writing by Women*, ed.s Sara-Mae Tuson, Chikodi Nwaiwu, Steph Pike & Agnes Meadows [Morgan's Eye Press, Spring 2014].

'We Will Not Be Deodorised' and 'Suffragette City' were first published in *Suffragette Legacy*, ed.s Camilla Mørk Røstik & Ella Louise Sutherland [Cambridge Scholars Publishing, 2015].

'Neon' was first published in *My Dear Watson: The Very Elements in Poetry*, ed. Rebecca Bilkau [Beautiful Dragons Press, 2015].